SandCastle™

Sports
By the Numbers

Bowling
By the Numbers

Desirée Bussiere

Consulting Editor, Diane Craig, M.A./Reading Specialist

A Division of ABDO

ABDO
Publishing Company

visit us at www.abdopublishing.com

Published by ABDO Publishing Company, a division of ABDO, P.O. Box 398166, Minneapolis, Minnesota 55439. Copyright © 2014 by Abdo Consulting Group, Inc. International copyrights reserved in all countries. No part of this book may be reproduced in any form without written permission from the publisher. SandCastle™ is a trademark and logo of ABDO Publishing Company.

Printed in the United States of America, North Mankato, Minnesota
062013
092013

 PRINTED ON RECYCLED PAPER

Editor: Liz Salzmann
Content Developer: Nancy Tuminelly
Cover and Interior Design and Production: Colleen Dolphin, Mighty Media
Cover Production: Kate Hartman
Photo Credits: iStockphoto/ Yenwen Lu, Shutterstock, Thinkstock

Library of Congress Cataloging-in-Publication Data

Bussiere, Desiree, 1989-
  Bowling by the numbers / Desiree Bussiere.
    pages cm. -- (Sports by the numbers)
  ISBN 978-1-61783-842-2
1. Bowling--Juvenile literature. 2. Numerals--Juvenile literature. I. Title.
  GV903.5.B87 2013
  794.6--dc23
                              2012049832

SandCastle™ Level: Transitional

SandCastle™ books are created by a team of professional educators, reading specialists, and content developers around five essential components—phonemic awareness, phonics, vocabulary, text comprehension, and fluency—to assist young readers as they develop reading skills and strategies and increase their general knowledge. All books are written, reviewed, and leveled for guided reading, early reading intervention, and Accelerated Reader® programs for use in shared, guided, and independent reading and writing activities to support a balanced approach to literacy instruction. The SandCastle™ series has four levels that correspond to early literacy development. The levels are provided to help teachers and parents select appropriate books for young readers.

Emerging Readers
(no flags)

Beginning Readers
(1 flag)

Transitional Readers
(2 flags)

Fluent Readers
(3 flags)

Contents

Introduction

Numbers are used all the time in bowling.

- A bowling lane has 10 pins.

- The **distance** between the foul line and the first pin is 60 feet (18.2 m).

- A bowling lane is 41 to 42 inches (104 to 107 cm) wide.

- Bowling balls weigh up to 16 pounds (7.3 kg).

- A bowling game has 10 frames.

Let's learn more about how numbers are used in bowling.

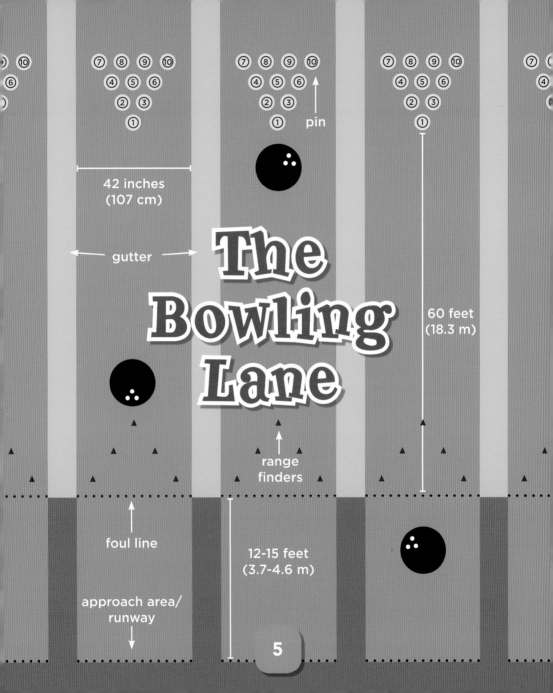

The Bowling Lane

7 8 9 10
4 5 6
2 3
1

7 8 9 10
4 5 6
2 3
1 pin

7 8 9 10
4 5 6
2 3
1

42 inches
(107 cm)

← gutter →

60 feet
(18.3 m)

▲ range
finders ▲

foul line

12-15 feet
(3.7-4.6 m)

approach area/
runway

The Sport

Each turn is called a frame. It **includes** up to two rolls.

The bowler rolls the ball toward the pins. He or she gets 1 point for each pin that falls down.

If the bowler **knocks** down all the pins, that's a strike. His or her turn is over.

If all the pins don't fall down, the bowler rolls a second time. If the second roll knocks the rest of the pins down, that's a spare.

Scoring

Add the number of pins **knocked** down by each roll together. That is the score for the frame.

Spares and strikes are worth 10 points. But bowlers get extra points for them too.

For a spare, add the points for the next roll.

For a strike, add the points for the next two rolls.

An "X" is used to mark a strike. A "/" is used to mark a spare. A "-" is used to mark a miss.

PLAYERS	1	2	3	4	5	6	7	8	9	10	TOTAL
Paul	6 2 — 8	7 / — 23	5 2 — 30	X — 49	8 1 — 58	4 3 — 65	4 4 — 73	9 - — 82	8 / — 98	6 3 — 107	107
Max	9 - — 9	7 1 — 17	9 / — 34	7 2 — 43	6 / — 62	9 / — 80	8 1 — 89	8 - — 97	3 2 — 102	6 - — 108	108
Jen	8 / — 13	3 5 — 21	8 - — 29	4 2 — 35	6 - — 41	4 / — 58	7 2 — 67	7 / — 84	7 / — 103	9 / 4 — 117	117
Ava	4 2 — 6	3 / — 19	3 5 — 27	7 - — 34	8 - — 42	4 3 — 49	3 5 — 57	5 2 — 64	7 - — 71	8 1 — 80	80

8

Paul likes to bowl. He uses a blue bowling ball.

By the Numbers!

A

Paul has bowled 5 frames. There are 10 frames in the game. How many frames does he have left?

(answer on p. 23)

Mary learns to bowl. She rolls the ball toward the pins.

By the Numbers!

B Mary's first roll **knocked** down 3 pins. Now she tries to knock down 7 more. How many pins would that be total?

(answer on p. 23)

Max is a good bowler. He can roll the ball very fast.

By the Numbers!

C

Max got 4 spares in the first game. He has 2 spares in this game. How many total spares does he have?

(answer on p. 23)

Jen is on a bowling team. Her team is the Bowler Girls.

By the Numbers!

D The Bowler Girls won 8 games. The other team won 6 games. How many more games did the Bowler Girls win?

(answer on p. 23)

16

Jacob bowls with his **parents**. They go every Sunday.

By the Numbers!

E

Jacob started bowling when he was 5. Now he is 9. How many years ago did he start?

(answer on p. 23)

18

Paige just bowled a strike!
She smiles and **cheers**.

By the Numbers!

F

Paige bowled 1 strike in this game. She bowled
2 strikes in the last game. How many total strikes
did she bowl?

(answer on p. 23)

David is waiting for his turn to bowl.

By the Numbers!

G David **knocked** down 7 pins in the first frame. He knocked down 4 pins in the second frame. What is his total score in the game?

(answer on p. 23)

Bowling Facts

- The highest bowling score is 300. It is a perfect game. It means the bowler got a strike every turn.

- Bowling 3 strikes in a row is called a turkey.

- Bowling pins are 15 inches (38 cm) tall.

- The largest **bowling alley** in the world is in Japan. It has 156 lanes.

- The WTBA World **Championships** were first held in 1954.

Answers to By the Numbers!

D

$$\begin{array}{r} 8 \\ -6 \\ \hline 2 \end{array}$$

The Bowler Girls won 8 games. The other team won 6 games. How many more games did the Bowler Girls win?

A

$$\begin{array}{r} 10 \\ -5 \\ \hline 5 \end{array}$$

Paul has bowled 5 frames. There are 10 frames in the game. How many frames does he have left?

E

$$\begin{array}{r} 9 \\ -5 \\ \hline 4 \end{array}$$

Jacob started bowling when he was 5. Now he is 9. How many years ago did he start?

B

$$\begin{array}{r} 3 \\ +7 \\ \hline 10 \end{array}$$

Mary's first roll **knocked** down 3 pins. Now she tries to knock down 7 more. How many pins would that be total?

F

$$\begin{array}{r} 1 \\ +2 \\ \hline 3 \end{array}$$

Paige bowled 1 strike in this game. She bowled 2 strikes in the last game. How many total strikes did she bowl?

C

$$\begin{array}{r} 4 \\ +2 \\ \hline 6 \end{array}$$

Max got 4 spares in the first game. He has 2 spares in this game. How many total spares does he have?

G

$$\begin{array}{r} 7 \\ +4 \\ \hline 11 \end{array}$$

David knocked down 7 pins in the first frame. He knocked down 4 pins in the second frame. What is his total score in the game?

Glossary

bowling alley – place with bowling lanes where people go to bowl.

championship – a series of games played to decide which team or player is the best.

cheer – to shout because you are happy about something.

distance – the amount of space between two places or things.

include – to take in as part of a group.

knock – to hit something with force.

parent – a mother or father.